# SMALL RAIN

# Small Rain

## VERSES FROM THE BIBLE

CHOSEN BY JESSIE ORTON JONES

ILLUSTRATED BY ELIZABETH ORTON JONES

New York : Published by The Viking Press : 1949

FIRST PUBLISHED NOVEMBER 1943

SECOND PRINTING APRIL 1944

THIRD PRINTING JULY 1944

FOURTH PRINTING SEPTEMBER 1944

FIFTH PRINTING JULY 1945

SIXTH PRINTING SEPTEMBER 1948

SEVENTH PRINTING NOVEMBER 1949

EIGHTH PRINTING APRIL 1951

NINTH PRINTING APRIL 1953

TENTH PRINTING NOVEMBER 1954

ELEVENTH PRINTING APRIL 1958

Lithographed in the United States of America by Reehl Litho Company

Published on the same day in the Dominion of Canada by
The Macmillan Company of Canada Limited

*Suffer the little children to come unto me, and forbid them not:*
*For of such is the kingdom of God.*

The heavens declare the glory of God;
And the firmament sheweth his handywork.

The earth is the Lord's and the fulness thereof;
The world, and they that dwell therein.

Let the heavens be glad, and let the earth rejoice:
And let men say among the nations, The Lord reigneth.

Make a joyful noise unto the Lord, all ye lands.

Serve the Lord with gladness:

Come before his presence with singing.

Know ye that the Lord he is God:

It is he that hath made us, and not we ourselves;

We are his people, and the sheep of his pasture.

Enter into his gates with thanksgiving,

And into his courts with praise:

Be thankful unto him, and bless his name,

For the Lord is good;

His mercy is everlasting;

And his truth endureth to all generations.

The trees of the Lord are full of sap;
    Where the birds make their nests.
He sendeth the springs into the valleys,
    Which run among the hills.
They give drink to every beast of the field.
He appointed the moon for seasons:
    The sun knoweth his going down.

O Lord my God, thou art very great;
Thou makest darkness, and it is night:
    Wherein all the beasts of the forest do creep forth.
The sun ariseth, they gather themselves together,
    And lay them down in their dens.
Man goeth forth unto his work
    And to his labour until the evening.
These wait all upon thee.
    Thou sendest forth thy spirit, they are created.

I will sing unto the Lord as long as I live:
    I will be glad in the Lord.

The Lord is my shepherd;

    I shall not want.

He maketh me to lie down in green pastures:

He leadeth me beside the still waters.

    He restoreth my soul:

He leadeth me in the paths of righteousness for his name's sake.

    Yea, though I walk through the valley of the shadow of death,

    I will fear no evil:

    For thou art with me;

Thy rod and thy staff they comfort me.

    Thou preparest a table before me

    In the presence of mine enemies:

    Thou anointest my head with oil;

    My cup runneth over.

Surely goodness and mercy shall follow me all the days of my life:

    And I will dwell in the house of the Lord for ever.

If I take the wings of the morning,
And dwell in the uttermost parts of the sea;
Even there shall thy hand lead me,
And thy right hand shall hold me.

But where shall wisdom be found?
  And where is the place of understanding?
God understandeth the way thereof,
  And he knoweth the place.

If any of you lack wisdom,
Let him ask of God . . .
And it shall be given him.

Every good gift and every perfect gift is from above,
And cometh down from the Father of lights.

There shall be showers of blessing.

Our Father which art in heaven,

Hallowed be thy name.

Thy kingdom come.

Thy will be done

In earth, as it is in heaven.


Give us this day our daily bread.

And forgive us our debts,

As we forgive our debtors.

And lead us not into temptation,

But deliver us from evil:

For thine is the kingdom, and the power,

And the glory, forever.


Amen.

My little children, let us not love in word,

Neither in tongue;

But in deed and in truth.

Be ye kind one to another,

Tenderhearted, forgiving one another.

All things whatsoever ye would that men should do to you,

Do ye even so to them.

Blessed shalt thou be in the city,
And blessed shalt thou be in the field.

Blessed shalt thou be when thou comest in,
And blessed shalt thou be when thou goest out.

I am but a little child:

I know not how to go out or come in.

Give therefore thy servant an understanding heart . . .

That I may discern between good and bad.

Search me, O God, and know my heart:

Try me, and know my thoughts:

And see if there be any wicked way in me,

And lead me in the way everlasting.

Blessed are the pure in heart: for they shall see God.

Blessed are the peacemakers: for they shall be called the children of God.

All of you are children of the most High.

He that dwelleth in the secret place of the most High
  Shall abide under the shadow of the Almighty.
I will say of the Lord, He is my refuge and my fortress:
  My God: in him will I trust.

For he shall give his angels charge over thee,
  To keep thee in all thy ways.
He shall cover thee with his feathers,
  And under his wings shalt thou trust.

He will not suffer thy foot to be moved:
  He that keepeth thee will not slumber.
The Lord shall preserve thee from all evil:
  He shall preserve thy soul.

The Lord shall preserve thy going out and thy coming in
From this time forth, and even for evermore.

The Lord is thy keeper.

The eternal God is thy refuge,

. . . and underneath are the everlasting arms.

# CITATIONS: